Parakeets

Cyril Rogers

P9-EDW-524

John Bartholomew & Son Limited
Edinburgh and London

© *John Bartholomew & Son Limited,* 1976
All Rights Reserved. No part of this publication may be reproduced, stored
in a retrieval system, or transmitted, in any form or by any means, electronic,
mechanical, photocopying, recording or otherwise, without the prior
permission of John Bartholomew & Son Limited.

ISBN 0 7028 1051 7

1st edition

Designed and illustrated by Allard Design Group Limited
Printed in Great Britain by W. S. Cowell Limited, Ipswich, Suffolk

Contents

4

Budgerigars and their care

In the first half of the nineteenth century European explorers were discovering new countries and bringing back strange and previously unseen animals, birds, plants, and flowers. One of these explorers, John Gould, an English ornithologist, carried out field work on birds in the then little-known Australia. He returned to England from one of his trips in 1840 with a collection of wild life, which included some light-green budgerigars, the very first examples to be seen alive in Europe, although some years earlier skins and coloured field drawings of budgerigars had been brought to Europe and the existence of the species recorded. The records of what happened after this first importation are somewhat hazy and incomplete and it is not known how many pairs of birds were actually involved. But it is quite clear that within a short space of time budgerigars were being bred with ease in captivity in several European countries.

Aviculturists found budgerigars a particularly attractive variety of parakeets. They were easy to breed in their natural, wild colouring and their production went on happily and freely for a number of years. Exploring ornithologists of that period identified two subspecies of budgerigars in addition to the main form, and all three kinds were undoubtedly included in the large consignments of budgerigars imported into Europe at various times. These three slightly differing kinds were blended together in the formation of the domesticated race of budgerigars, which accounts for the small variations seen today in different strains.

Between the years 1870 and 1875, Yellow mutations occurred in several European countries, the first being recorded in Germany. There were in fact two distinct Yellow mutations, the ordinary suffused Yellow and the pure Yellow with red eyes (Lutinos). The ordinary Yellows were soon established in several strains, but the red-eyed kind disappeared — not to be seen again until many years later when a further mutation occurred. Most probably the reason why the first mutation of red-eyed Yellows (Lutinos) was not established was through lack of knowledge on the part of their owners. Ornithologists had noted few examples of Yellow birds flying with wild flocks of Light Greens in Australia. The appearance of Yellow birds amongst Green parakeets is not an unusual feature, and occurs with many kinds. Since there are no sure records of any wild-caught Yellow Birds being trapped and used for breeding in aviaries it seems likely that all the Yellows must have been mutations bred in captivity. It was from these first strains of suffused Yellows that British breeders evolved the richly coloured Buttercup Yellows in the early 1900s. These Buttercup Yellows played a big part in popularizing budgerigars as cage and aviary birds and yet, at present, examples are rarely seen.

After the appearance of the Yellow mutations breeders began to speculate on what would be the next mutation (bearing in mind that green is a mixture of blue and yellow). Sure enough, in 1880 blue-coloured budgerigars were reported as having been bred in Holland. Little was known about this mutation and it apparently disappeared from aviaries. Blue budgerigars were not heard of again until many years later, this time in Belgium. The breeder there kept the strain very much to himself whilst it was being developed and until 1910 Sky Blue budgerigars had not been seen in Great Britain. During that year they were exhibited at a large cage bird show in London where they created quite a sensation. The appearance of these beautifully coloured birds caused the cage-bird world to think that budgerigars were something special in respect of their colourings, and enthusiasm was kindled in many keepers of parrot-like birds. For nearly a decade Sky Blues were in the aviaries of a very limited number of experienced aviculturists who thought them rather delicate, expensive, and more difficult to breed than the commoner Light Greens and Yellows. The arrival of the Sky Blues meant that budgerigars were available in two ground colours, and it was possible with each mutation for two sets of colours to be produced.

It was in the aviary of a British breeder, in 1920, that the first White Sky Blue birds were bred in a mixed collection of Light Greens, Sky Blues and Light Yellows. It was then realized that these White birds were in fact the Blue form of the Yellows, although at the time the rules of their inheritance were not clear to the breeders. Prior to the arrival of the Whites an important mutation had occurred in France in 1915 at a large commercial budgerigar-breeding establishment. It is generally accepted that this Dark Green, Laurel Green, or Satin Green mutation did occur in these French aviaries. Nevertheless, it is known that at least one Dark Green had been bred amongst the wild Green flocks in Australia and there is a skin from such a bird in the Natural History Museum, London. This indicates that it was possible for a Dark Green bird to have been imported from Australia along with a batch of wild-caught Light Greens.

A year after the first Dark Greens had been bred in captivity a

Map of South Asia — Australia   Origins of Budgerigars

further green shade — the Olive Green — was produced. These Olive Greens were bred by pairing together two Dark Green birds. With the knowledge we have today this was something that was to be expected. At that time, however, it came as a complete surprise. The breeding of the Olive Greens meant that there were now three shades of the green colouring and correspondingly the shades of blue, white, and yellow were each also obtainable in three shades, making a total of twelve colours.

The Blue counterparts of the Dark Greens were originally referred to as Dark Blue, Powder Blue, and Cobalt Blue but eventually settled under the name of Cobalt. Blue forms of the Olive Greens were called Lilacs, Lavenders, and Mauves according to the individual breeder's preference but eventually Mauve became their universal name. Between 1918 and 1925, the time of the first breedings of the Dark Greens and the Whites, there were several reports of pale-green-coloured birds with brownish-grey undulations. These were usually called Apple Greens or Jades according to their particular shade. These birds were generally described by most breeders, who had not actually seen them, as being just badly coloured Yellows.

In 1925 an Apple Green appeared as a mutation in my aviaries and, being interested in colour breeding, I decided to carry out breeding experiments to discover the true position of these birds. During the next few years a number of other examples of Apple Greens were gathered together from various sources and several strains of true breeding birds evolved. When in 1928 the Blue form of the Apple Green was discovered in Germany a much wider interest was taken in this variety. In due course the Apple Greens and their German Blue counterparts were recognized as being the same mutation and ultimately given the group name of Greywings.

While the Greywings were becoming increasingly popular both as exhibition and aviary birds a new and very strikingly coloured mutation appeared. This was in 1931 and the first examples of these new birds were hens. It surprised their breeder that when these hens were paired with Greywings of similar colouring all their young were normally coloured. After considerable investigation and numerous test pairings it was concluded that these birds were Cinnamons, and sex-linked in their breeding behaviour. At first they were named Cinnamonwings because of the brownish colouring of their wing markings. It was later discovered that they could be bred in all the known forms. Their name was then changed to Cinnamon and used as a prefix. These Cinnamons were the first mutation of the sex-linked kind to be established, and since then further similar mutations have appeared in Europe, Australia, America, and South Africa.

In the same year that the Cinnamons appeared, another rather unusually coloured mutation occurred in an aviary in California, America. This time the birds had brownish wing undulations, pallid body colours, and red eyes. Unfortunately they died out before they could be perpetuated. The following season a similar mutation occurred in Germany and fortunately was quickly established in a range of green and blue shades. Because their colours were not fully developed this group received the name of Fallow (used in the same sense as a 'fallow field' i.e. not cultivated). Because of their unique colouring and red eyes they were soon in demand by breeders and exhibitors and some very beautifully coloured examples of Fallows were produced. For some years they were in a prominent position in the budgerigar world and they held this position until about 1940 when their popularity sharply declined due to wartime conditions. By the late 1960s Fallows had almost disappeared from bird rooms and aviaries but through the efforts of a few keen colour breeders the mutation began once more to reestablish itself. New mutations occurred in Australia and Great Britain not long after the German Fallow mutation had been established. The colouring of the British Fallow is similar to that of the German Fallow, the only exception being the eyes which are solid bright red without the light iris ring which the German Fallows possess. Several other Fallow mutations have been reported but little is known about their hereditary behaviour or how the strains have been developed.

During the year in which the German Fallows came into being a further red-eyed race of birds was reported both in Germany and in Great Britain. These birds were clear white and clear yellow in colour with red eyes like the German Fallows. But it was only the German mutation that finally became established both in the red-eyed Yellow (Lutino) and red-eyed White (Albino) forms. Another Lutino mutation occurred in Great Britain in 1936. This time it was fully developed and became integrated with the established form. At first there were a few complications with the German Albinos and Lutinos as not merely one but two separate mutations had taken place, both coloured alike but with different hereditary behaviour. One kind was sex-linked like the Cinnamons and the other non sex-linked like the Greywings. When paired together the resulting colour of the chicks was not as would have been expected. This problem was resolved when it was discovered that the Laws of Mendelian Inheritance could be applied to budgerigars.

During the late 1920s and the early 1930s Dr Hans Duncker and Consul General Carl Cremer of Bremen conducted a large number of controlled crossbreeding experiments. The results of these experiments showed how the principles discovered by Gregor Mendel were applicable to budgerigars. In due course the book of *Budgerigar Matings* was published by the Budgerigar Society and it was through this book that the facts of budgerigar genetics became known world-wide. Prior to the discovery of Mendelian inheritance the breeding of the various colours of budgerigars was carried out on a very unscientific basis. The early breeders did sterling work in developing the new colour mutations but undoubtedly they could have achieved their objectives far quicker had they known more precisely how budgerigar colours were passed on from one generation to another.

With an ever-increasing number of colour mutations budgerigar culture spread in popularity throughout Europe, Australia, North America, Africa, and Asia. At the 1925 Crystal Palace Exhibition of Cage Birds held in London a group of budgerigar enthusiasts

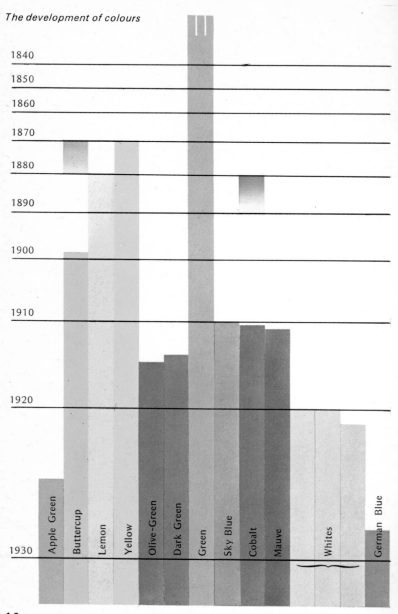

The development of colours

1840

1850

1860

1870

1880

1890

1900

1910

1920

Apple Green
Buttercup
Lemon
Yellow
Olive-Green
Dark Green
Green
Sky Blue
Cobalt
Mauve
Whites
German Blue

1930

10

	1930	1932	1934	1936	1938	1940	1942	1944	1946	1948
Continental Clearflights										
Australian Pied										
Danish Recessive Pied										
Clearwing										
Opaline										
Fallow										
Cinnamon										
Yellows										
Greens										
Blues										
Whites										
Greywings										
Lutino/Albino										
Dominant Grey										
English Recessive Grey										
Slate										
Yellowface Blue										
Violet										
Lacewing										

11

gathered together and formed the Budgerigar Club. From a small beginning the Club developed into The Budgerigar Society which today has thousands of members from all countries, and has under its jurisdiction many National Specialist and Area Societies. It is quite certain that without the numerous colour mutations and the fine work of The Budgerigar Society in their development, budgerigars would not have had such an impact on the cage-bird fancy as a whole.

Colour mutations continued to appear, but it was in 1933 that the first of the colour-pattern mutations occurred simultaneously in Great Britain, Europe, and Australia. The British mutation occurred in a breeder's aviary in Scotland, the Australian race evolved from a wild-caught specimen, but the origin of the European one does not seem to have been recorded. The British mutation started with a cobalt-coloured hen and was first known as Marbled and Pied. The Australian strain was called Opaline. It was found that all three mutations were due to one basic character, the third in the sex-linked series, and the Australian name was universally adopted as being the most suitable. These Opalines quickly became very popular and were bred in many different bright colours and combinations of colours. It will be seen in the chapter on Descriptions of Colour how very beautiful some of these Opaline forms can be. At this period Australia played an important rôle in the discovery of mutations and soon after the success of the Opalines they produced the Clearwings and Dominant Greys. The group name 'Clearwings' covers the vividly coloured Yellow-wing Green series and White-wing Blue series and does not indicate a separate variety. Clearwings were second in the patterned character series. They are recessive in their hereditary behaviour to normal colours and dominant to the Yellow and White kind.

The colour of the Dominant Australian Greys is caused, not by a colour character as such, but by a character which prevents the blue from forming in the birds' plumage. Its presence changes all the blue colours into various shades of grey, and all the green colours into shades of dull grey-green. As the name indicates, the character is a dominant one and appears to be the first of the Dominant muta-tions. Whilst the dominant Australian Greys were being developed a further Grey mutation appeared in Great Britain; this time a recessive one. These recessive Greys were a shade or two deeper in their general colouring than the dominant kind and like them could be had in all the Green and Blue varieties. The dominant Australian Greys became very popular and are still sought after today. The recessive Greys, however, had little success and disappeared from breeders' aviaries during the Second World War. Just prior to the appearance of the English recessive Greys another similarly coloured type was bred. This time it was known as Slate and was a further sex-linked variety. The addition of the Slate character changed the colour of the Blue birds into a slate-blue shade of varying depths according to the blue shade to which it was added. Slates were never very popular, perhaps because they appeared at the same time as the sought-after Dominant Greys. Nevertheless, Slates have persisted and there are still a number of examples.

Birds with broken plumage had been recorded from time to time but it was not until about 1933 that a true breeding strain of pied birds appeared in Denmark. These birds were either green broken with clear yellow or blue broken with areas of clear white. They are recessive in their manner of inheritance and are usually known as Danish Recessive Pieds, but are sometimes called Harlequins in America. The eyes of the Danish Recessive Pieds differ from all the other varieties in that they are a deep solid plum colour without the usual light iris ring. It is by this eye colour that all the different varieties of Danish Recessive Pieds can be positively identified. The first examples of the Danish Recessive Pieds were not seen in Great Britain until 1948. As the Pied forms were being established in Denmark another Pied mutation occurred in Australia. This mutation differed from the Danish Pied not only in its markings but also in breeding behaviour. The Dominant Australian Pieds, as they were called, did not appear in Great Britain until the early 1950s although breeders had long been aware of their existence. Being Dominants they were much easier to breed and improve in overall quality than the Recessive kind and quickly superseded them in popularity.

A third Pied type, the Dominant Continental Clearflighted, was developed in Belgium during that country's wartime occupation, and examples found their way into Great Britain during 1946-47. For a short time they were bred freely in most colours, and many well-marked specimens were produced both in Britain and Europe. When the Dominant Australian Pieds appeared they quickly outpaced the Clearflighted and at the present time only a very few examples are bred each year. But the Clearflighteds have another value: when combined with the Danish Recessive Pied character they produce the Dark-eyed Clear birds. These are birds with the same coloured eyes as the Danish Recessive Pieds, but with pure-white or pure-yellow plumage. In fact they are the only really pure-coloured White and Yellow budgerigars.

In 1936-37 the lovely Violet mutation occurred simultaneously in Australia, Denmark, and Great Britain. The British Violet mutation was a recessive one and only existed for a short time before the strain died out, faced with strong competition from the Dominant Violet variety. Both the Australian and Danish Violets are dominants and it is from them that all the present-day Violet strains are descended. The Violet character resembles the Dominant Grey character in that its presence alters the blue or green colours carried by the birds. This beautiful deep-violet colour is only visible when the birds also have a single character for Dark in their genetic make up. Violet-coloured birds are most fascinating to breed and can be obtained in all the other existing varieties.

It was always thought impossible for budgerigars to have both yellow and white feathers in their plumage at the same time, but in the mid-1930s the Yellow-faced Blue mutation appeared in Great Britain, Europe, Australia, and America. There are several distinct mutations of this Yellow-faced Blue manifestation with varying amounts of yellow, each having different ways of inheritance. To date only two forms of Yellow-faced Blues have been fully investigated and they are identified as Mutant I and Mutant II. A third deeply coloured Yellow or Golden-faced form, as it is usually called, is now being examined in detail and its breeding behaviour is steadily becoming much clearer.

In 1948 the fifth member of the sex-linked group of varieties appeared in Great Britain. It is the only mutation to be recorded in the last 30 years. These birds have the red eyes of the sex-linked Albinos and Lutinos. The bodies are generally white or yellow with light cinnamon-brown throat spots, undulations, and tail markings. It was suggested by some breeders that the Lacewings, as these birds are called, could be bred by crossing the Cinnamon and Albino or Lutino characters together. This theory was soon shown to be quite incorrect, and it was discovered that the Lacewings were a separate variety. This idea was undoubtedly prompted by the fact that it is possible to have Lacewing kinds of all the other varieties. The Lacewing forms of the Yellows or Whites superficially resemble ordinary Lutinos or Albinos.

American breeders have produced a variety known as Clearbodies which have dark markings and dark tails with clear-white or clear-yellow bodies. Their pattern markings are quite different from those of the Clearwings and it would make an interesting experiment to cross these two forms. This may be possible when the Clearbodies are more readily available in Great Britain. A similar variety has appeared in Australia; these birds have grey wing markings and clear-white or clear-yellow bodies. These Greywing Yellows and Greywing Whites have not been officially recorded outside Australia. Odd specimens have been reported in mixed aviary collections but have not become established in the same way as the Australian variety.

All the mutations so far discussed have been connected with colour. However, there have been three mutations which have influenced the feathers themselves; they are the Longflighted, Crests, and excessive-frilling mutations. Events have shown that it is only the Crested forms that are acceptable to breeders. The Longflighteds were an ugly narrow shape with very long flight and tail feathers which made it difficult for them to fly properly. For a time they were used by some exhibition breeders to introduce certain good features they had into normal strains. Some success was achieved in this respect, but in the end the Longflighted birds were barred from shows, and have now more or less disappeared. The birds with excessive frilling were eventually allowed to die out as their long, curling feathers inhibited both flight and reproduction.

The Crests, on the other hand, have been developed and both of the mutations, one from France and the other from North America, are of the same genetic kind. Crests exist in all colour varieties and with three different shapes of crests — the Full Circular, the Half Circular, and the Tufted. It is the same character but with different modifiers that causes these three different types of Crested birds to appear. Although the character for Crests is a dominant one the number and type of crests produced are controlled by the modifiers carried by the individual specimens. Crests do not appeal to all budgerigar fanciers, but those who do favour them find Crest breeding particularly interesting.

The budgerigar fancy can be roughly divided into three sections, all interdependent on each other's activities — the exhibition breeders, the colour breeders, and the pet owners. Exhibiting breeders improve the overall quality of the various colours produced by the efforts of the colour breeders. The surplus birds from both of these sections are absorbed by the pet-bird keepers. At some of the large exhibitions of cage birds the entries in the budgerigar sections will frequently total several thousand and it can well be imagined what a beautiful sight they make. At smaller shows there are usually some hundreds of budgerigars of all colours on view. Mixed with the other varieties of cage birds they make a delightful

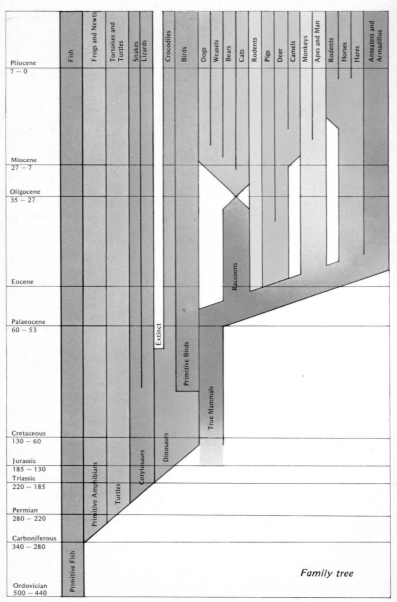

Family tree

16

display of colour and song. Colour breeders frequently show their rare colour specimens at these shows thereby adding an even greater variety of colour. Some fanciers keep budgerigars solely for decorative purposes and they certainly do make a cheerful and colourful display at all times of the year. An aviary of mixed coloured budgerigars will always make a pretty garden even more attractive.

As pets for a family or a single person, budgerigars are ideal, being easy to house, keep, and feed. They will become very tame and many specimens will learn to imitate the human voice and other sounds. I think that it can be said without fear of contradiction that these delightful little domesticated Australian parakeets have given and still give more pleasure to more people than any other species of cage bird.

For schools and other educational establishments budgerigars are excellent subjects for explaining simple and easily understood genetics. It is fascinating for young people to be able to see the actual process of inheritance by carrying out crossbreeding experiments for themselves, watching the different colours hatch and develop in the nests.

Description of colours

The previous chapter outlined how and when the many different colour mutations appeared amongst the stocks of budgerigars in various parts of the world. This chapter will give colour descriptions of these beautiful birds so that the varieties can be recognized when seen. This book contains an outline drawing of a budgerigar on which various parts of the bird are marked so that the reader can refer to the diagram while reading the detailed colour descriptions.

Budgerigars can be divided into two groups of basic ground colours on which all other colours are superimposed; these basic colours are yellow and white. Birds having the yellow ground colour are commonly known as Green-series birds and those with the white, Blue-series, to which can be added the Yellow-faced Blue kind. The next grouping of colours is done by the depth of the colours seen on the basic ground colours and then followed by the pattern markings. In the budgerigar fancy it is usual to call the older mutations normal colours and the later ones rare, or unusual, colours although there is no definite ruling laid down by any society as to the line of demarcation.

The first descriptions I shall give are those which are generally considered to belong to the Normal group starting with the original Light Green.

Light Green also known as Green, Normal Green, and Wild Type Green, has a clear, bright-yellow forehead and facial area (mask) which is ornamented on each side of the face with violet-blue cheek patches (flashes). On the lower part of the mask there are six round black throat spots, one on each side being partially hidden by the cheek patch. From the mask to the base of the tail, including the rump, flanks, and thighs, the colour is a bright grass green. On the back of the head, neck, mantle, back, and wings there are black undulating markings which stand out clearly against the yellow ground. The flight feathers are blackish with some greenish

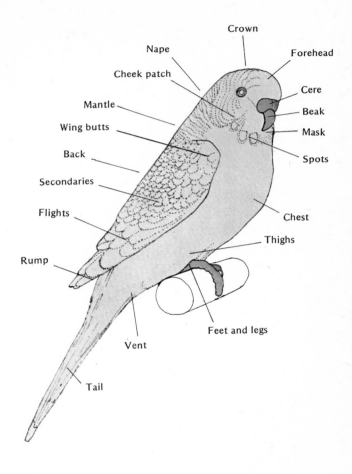

Crown

Forehead

Nape

Cere

Cheek patch

Beak

Mantle

Mask

Wing butts

Spots

Back

Secondaries

Chest

Flights

Thighs

Rump

Feet and legs

Vent

Tail

Anatomical parts

Light Green

suffusion. The two long central tail feathers are very dark blue, the remainder yellow with dark pattern markings. The beak of the Light Green budgerigar is horn-coloured; the feet and legs range from pinkish flesh-coloured to dark blue.

The Dark Green and Olive Green forms are marked like the Light Green except for their body colours and a slight deepening of the yellow ground. Dark Green has a rich, dark-green tone similar to that of the laurel shrub and was at one time called Laurel Green. The shade of the Olive Green is quite different: it is a softer, sandy green like ripe olives. These three green colours are carried in a different depth of tone by all the other Green-series birds.

The Blue counterpart of the Light Green is known as Blue, Light Blue, Azure Blue, and Sky Blue; Sky Blue is the official and most

Dark Green

Olive-Green

Greens

generally used name. Sky Blue has a pure-white forehead and mask, ornamented on each side of the face with violet-blue cheek patches. On the lower part of the mask there are six round black throat spots, one on each side being partially hidden by the cheek patch. From the mask to the base of the tail, including the rump, flanks, and thighs, the colour is bright sky blue. On the back of the head, neck, mantle, back, and wings are black undulating markings clear-cut on a white ground. The flight feathers are blackish with some blue suffusion and the two long central tail feathers are deep blue. The remainder are white with dark pattern markings. The beak of the Sky Blue is horn-coloured and the feet and legs range from pink to dark blue.

The Cobalt and Mauve forms are marked like the Sky Blue but with rich cobalt-blue and greyish-mauve body colours respectively. Although the shade and depth of the cobalt does vary slightly with individual strains it is in the mauve that the greatest variation can be found. At one time Mauve was also known as Lilac and Lavender because of the difference of the shade but now the lighter, warmer shades have given way to the greyish-mauve colour. These three Blue colour shades will be found repeated in different intensities in the other Blue-series birds.

Sky Blue

Cobalt

Mauve

23

Light Yellow
(light suffusion)

The ordinary Light Yellow is included in the Normal group together with Dark Yellow and Olive Yellow. These Light Yellow birds are divided into two kinds, those which are nearly pure yellow (light suffusion) and those which carry varying degrees of green suffusion (deep suffusion). Light Yellow (light suffusion) is a rich bright yellow throughout with just traces of ghost undulations on back of head, neck, mantle, back, and wings. Faint throat spots may or may not be present. The cheek patches can be silvery-white, or silvery-white with a light pinkish-violet flush. Flight and tail feathers are whitish-yellow with the beak yellow horn-coloured and the feet and legs pink or blue. Light Yellow of deep suffusion has a distinct light-green suffusion on body with light greyish throat spots and undulating markings on back of head, neck, back, mantle, and wings. The cheek patches are light bluish-violet and the long tail feathers are heavily suffused with blue. The beak is yellow horn-coloured and the feet and legs are mostly blue but can be pinkish according to their breeding.

The Dark Yellow and Olive Yellow forms can again be had in both light and deep suffusions, the latter being more common. Both of these are coloured like the Light Yellow except that their body suffusions are dark green and pale olive-green with an overall deepening of the yellow colouring.

Dark Yellow
(dark suffusion)

Olive-Yellow
(deep suffusion)

Yellows

Like the Yellow shades the White Sky Blue, White Cobalt, and White Mauve, of both depths of suffusion, are considered to be Normals. At the present time it is the Whites of deep suffusion that are most common, and the light-suffused kind are very rare. White Sky Blue of light suffusion should be like the Light Yellow except that the yellow shade is replaced by white with faint bluish cast. It is the White Mauve that most frequently has the purest colour.

White Sky Blue of deep suffusion is a most attractive form being light sky blue with light greyish throat spots and undulating markings on back of head, neck, mantle, back, and wings. The cheek patches are light bluish-violet, and the long tail feathers heavily suffused with blue. The beak of the White Sky Blue is yellow horn-colour, and the feet and legs are pinkish to blue.

The White Cobalt and White Mauve of deep suffusion are marked like the White Sky Blue except for the change of body shade to bright light cobalt and light mauve. Because Whites of deep suffusion sometimes have quite heavy undulating markings they are wrongly called Greywings. The undulating markings of both suffusions of the Whites are narrow, whereas those of the Greywing kinds are wide, and of a more pure grey colour.

Sky-Blue White

Cobalt-White

Mauve-White

I have discussed the Normal Green, Blue, Yellow, and White forms in their three body shades. Now comes a further Normal variety where the body colouring is midway between green and yellow — the Greywing Green and blue and white — the Greywing Sky Blue. The name Greywing is always used as a prefix.

Greywing Light Green has a clear yellow forehead and mask which is ornamented on each side of the face with pale lilac-blue cheek patches. On the lower part of the mask there are six round brownish-grey throat spots, one on each side being partially hidden by the cheek patch. From the mask to the base of the tail, including the rump, flanks, and thighs, the colour is the pale soft green of young beech leaves. On the back of head, neck, mantle, back, and wings are smokey brownish-grey undulating markings on a pale-yellow ground. The flight feathers are coloured like the markings, and the two long central tail feathers are pale blue with the remainder pale yellow with brownish-grey pattern markings. The beak of the Greywing Light Green is horn-coloured and the feet and legs are deep pink to blue.

The Greywing Dark Green and Greywing Olive Green are both marked like the Greywing Light Green except that their body colours are soft pale dark green and soft pale olive-green with somewhat of an orange-yellow shade. The yellow areas of both of these kinds are of a rather richer shade, particularly so with the Greywing Olive Green.

Greywing Sky Blue has the forehead and mask pure white and this is ornamented on each side of the face with soft lilac-blue cheek patches. On the lower part of the mask there are six round grey throat spots, one on each side being partially hidden by the cheek patch. From the mask to the base of the tail including the rump, flanks, and thighs, the colour is clear pale sky blue. On the back of head, neck, mantle, back, and wings are pure-grey undulating markings clear-cut on a white ground. The flight feathers are also pure grey and the two central tail feathers are dull blue with the remainder white with some medium-grey pattern markings. The beak of the Greywing Sky Blue is horn-coloured and the feet and legs range from pinkish flesh colour to dull blue.

The Greywing Cobalt and Greywing Mauve are marked like the Greywing Sky Blue except for the change of body shade to soft light cobalt and soft greyish-mauve. With all the Greywing kinds the markings of the cock birds are inclined to be a slightly darker grey than those of the hen birds.

Light-Green
Greywing

Sky-Blue
Greywing

Greywings

Since the Grey Greens and Grey Blues have become so popular they are now included in the Normal Group. There is a Grey Green form of the three green shades: all have the same body colour in different depths of shade.

Grey Light Green, usually known as Light Grey Green, has the forehead and mask dull light yellow and this is ornamented on each side of the face with silvery-grey cheek patches. On the lower part of the mask are six round black throat spots, one on each side is partially hidden by the cheek patch. From the mask to the base of tail, including the rump, flanks, and thighs, the colour is dull mustard-green. On the back of head, neck, mantle, back, and wings are jet-black undulating markings on a pale-yellow ground. The flight feathers and two long central tail feathers are jet black. The beak of the Light Grey Green is horn-coloured and the feet and legs are bluish-pink to greyish-blue.

The Grey Dark Green (medium Grey Green) and the Grey Olive Green (dark Grey Green) are marked like the Light Grey Green but have a correspondingly deeper body colour. There can be a Grey Green form of all the previously mentioned Green series.

The Grey Blue (light grey), mostly called just Grey, has the forehead and mask white and this is ornamented on each side of the face with silvery-grey cheek patches. On the lower part of the mask are six round black throat spots, one on each side is partially hidden by the cheek patch. From the mask to the base of the tail, including the rump, flanks, and thighs, the colour is dull battleship grey. On back of head, neck, mantle, back, and wings are jet-black undulating markings standing out clearly on a white ground. The flight feathers and two long central tail feathers are jet black. The beak of the Light Grey is horn-coloured and the feet and legs are bluish-pink to greyish-blue.

The Grey Cobalt (medium Grey) and Grey Mauve (dark Grey) are coloured like the Light Grey but with correspondingly deeper body colour. There can be a Grey form of all the previously mentioned Blue-series birds.

It seems to be contradictory to call birds Violet Greens when their colour is in fact green. But in these cases it is used to show that the altered green shade carried by the birds is due to the presence of the Violet character in their genetic make up. The word Violet is used as a prefix for all varieties having the character which is only visible as a true violet colour when certain other characters are also present.

Dark-Green Grey

Cobalt-Grey

Greys

Violet Light Green has the forehead and mask rich deep yellow and this is ornamented on each side of the face with dark-violet cheek patches. On the lower part of the mask are six round black throat spots, one on each side is partially hidden by the cheek patch. From the mask to the base of the tail, including the rump, flanks, and thighs, the colours are bright pale dark green. On the back of head, neck, mantle, back, and wings are black undulating markings on a deep-yellow ground. The flight feathers are blackish with some greenish suffusion and the two long central tail feathers are dark blue with the remainder rich yellow with dark pattern markings. The beak of the Violet Light Green is horn-coloured and the feet and legs are dark bluish.

The Violet Dark Green is marked similarly to the Violet Light Green except that the body colour is a hard even dull dark green, quite unlike the bright shade of the ordinary Dark Green. The Violet Olive Green is again similarly marked but here the body shade is extremely dark and is in fact the darkest of the green shades. The precise shade is hard to describe but it is somewhere between that of the Dark Green and Olive Green but very deep and solid. There can be a Violet Green form of all the previously mentioned Green series.

Violet Sky Blue has the forehead and mask white and this is ornamented on each side of the face with deep-violet cheek patches. On the lower part of the mask there are six round black throat spots, one on each side is partially hidden by the cheek patch. From the mask to the base of the tail, including the rump, flanks, and thighs, the colour is bright pale cobalt with a violet tone. On the back of head, neck, mantle, back, and wings are black undulating markings clear-cut on a white ground. The flight feathers are blackish with some violet-blue suffusion and the two long central tail feathers are very dark bright blue with the remainder white with dark pattern markings. The beak of the Violet Sky Blue is horn-coloured and the feet and legs bluish.

The Violet Cobalt, also known as Violet and Visual Violet, is marked like the Violet Sky Blue except that the body is a beautiful vivid violet shade. This is considered to be the most beautiful colour of all the many budgerigar forms and it is one that can be had in all the other varieties. Violet Cobalt is marked like the Violet Sky Blue except for the change of body colour to a rich deep violet. The particular shade of the violet can vary from bluish-violet to reddish-violet according to the strain. With the Violet Mauve the body colour is a violet-tinted mauve with some flecking of true violet

Light-Green
Violet

Mauve-Violet

Violets

33

feathers, particularly on the rump area. They are generally considered to be more pleasing to the eye than the ordinary greyish Mauves.

I now come to the first of the patterned varieties — the Opalines. There can be an Opaline form of all the other varieties both in the Green and Blue series. Some of these are considered to be Normals when they are the Opaline forms of the ordinary Normal kind. Opaline Light Green has the forehead and mask light yellow and this is ornamented on each side of the face with violet cheek patches. On the lower part of the mask are six round black throat spots, one on each side partially hidden by the cheek patch. From the mask to the base of the tail, including the rump, flanks, and thighs, the colour is very bright grass green. On the base of the head and neck the undulating markings are fine dark grey on a yellow ground with the mantle area practically free from markings and of the same bright-green colour as the body. The markings on the wings are wide and heavily suffused with bright green. The flight feathers are blackish with a light patch in the centre and are suffused with bright green. The two long central tail feathers are light yellowish in the centre surrounded by dark blue. The other feathers are yellow with dark pattern markings. The beak of the Opaline Light Green is horn-coloured, and the feet and legs range from pink to flesh colour and blue.

The Opaline Dark Green and Opaline Olive Green are marked like the Opaline Light Green except that their body colours and suffusions are bright dark green and rich warm olive-green.

Opaline Sky Blue has a white forehead and mask and this is ornamented on each side of the face with violet cheek patches. On the lower part of the mask there are six round black throat spots, one on each side being partially hidden by the cheek patch. From the mask to the base of the tail, including the rump, flanks, and thighs, the colour is bright clear sky blue. On back of the head and neck the undulating markings are fine and dark grey on a white ground. The mantle area is practically free from markings and of the same bright sky-blue shade as the body. The markings on the wings are wide and heavily suffused with bright sky blue. The flights are blackish in colour with a light patch in the centre and suffused with blue. The two long central feathers are whitish in the centre and surrounded by dark blue. The beak of the Opaline Sky Blue is horn-coloured and the feet and legs range from pink to flesh colour and blue.

Light-Green
Opaline

Sky-Blue
Opaline

Opalines

35

The Opaline Cobalt and Opaline Mauve are coloured like the Opaline Sky Blue except that their body colours and suffusions are bright cobalt and clear greyish-mauve.

Linking the Yellows and Whites with the Greywings is a patterned variety called by the group name of Clearwing. This includes Yellow-wing Greens and Whitewing Blues. Yellow-wing Light Green has a yellow forehead and mask which is ornamented on each side of the face with deep-violet-blue cheek patches. The lower part of the mask may, or may not, have six round greyish throat spots. From the mask to the base of the tail, including rump, flanks, and thighs, the colour is bright but light grass green. Back of head, neck, mantle, back, and wings are rich yellow, practically free from markings. The flight feathers are lighter yellow and the two long central tail feathers are blue. The beak of the Yellow-wing Light Green is horn-coloured and the feet and legs are pinkish or bluish.

The Yellow-wing Dark Green and Yellow-wing Olive Green are marked like the Yellow-wing Light Green except for the change of body shade to rich dark green and dark olive-green. The yellow on the wings of both of these is correspondingly richer.

Whitewing Sky Blue has a white forehead and mask which is ornamented on each side of the face with deep-violet-blue cheek patches. The lower part of the mask may, or may not, have six round greyish throat spots. From the mask to the base of the tail, including rump, flanks, and thighs, the colour is bright sky blue. Back of head, neck, mantle, back, and wings are clear white, as free as possible from markings. The two long central tail feathers are blue. The beak of the Whitewing Sky Blue is horn-coloured and the feet and legs are pinkish or bluish.

The Whitewing Cobalt and White Mauve are marked like the Whitewing Sky Blue except for the change of body colour to bright cobalt and bright greyish-mauve. The white on the wings of both these varieties sometimes shows more markings than the White-wing Sky Blue.

Like the Opalines some of the Cinnamons are considered to be Normals when they are the Cinnamon form of the ordinary Normal kind. Cinnamon Light Green has a pale-yellow forehead and mask which is ornamented on each side of the face with soft light-violet cheek patches. On the lower part of the mask there are six round, cinnamon-brown throat spots, one on each side being partially

Yellow/Light-Green
Clearwing

White/Sky-Blue
Clearwing

Clearwings

hidden by the cheek patch. From the mask to the base of the tail, including the rump, flanks, and thighs, the colour is pale soft light green. On the back of head, neck, mantle, back, and wings are cinnamon-brown undulating markings and the two long central tail feathers are bluish with a strong cinnamon tone, while the remainder are pale yellow with cinnamon-brown pattern markings. The beak of the Cinnamon Light Green is yellowish horn-colour and the feet and legs are pink.

The Cinnamon Dark Green and Cinnamon Olive Green are both marked like the Cinnamon Light Green with the exception that their body colours are soft dark green and pale olive-green with a distinct orange-yellow undertone. The yellow areas of both of these kinds are of a rich shade, particularly so with the Cinnamon Olive Green.

Cinnamon Sky Blue has a white forehead and mask which is ornamented on each side of the face with soft lilac cheek patches. On the lower part of the mask there are six round cinnamon-grey throat spots, one on each side being partially hidden by the cheek patch. From the mask to the base of the tail, including rump, flank, and thighs, the colour is pale sky blue. On the back of the head, neck, mantle, back, and wings are cinnamon-brown undulating markings on a white ground. The flight feathers are cinnamon-brown like the markings, and the two long central tail feathers are bluish with a strong cinnamon tone; the remainder are white with cinnamon-brown pattern markings. The beak of the Cinnamon Sky Blue is yellowish horn-colour and the feet and legs are pink.

The Cinnamon Cobalt and Cinnamon Mauve are both marked like the Cinnamon Sky Blue with the exception that their body colours are soft pale cobalt and soft violet-tinted mauve. The white areas of both kinds are clear which makes the markings appear to be darker than they really are. With some of these birds there is a strong tendency to a violet undertone which makes their colour particularly attractive.

The next patterned variety is the Dominant Pied, also known as Australian Dominant Pied, and Australian Banded Pied. This last name is given to specially marked birds. Dominant Pied Light Green is marked and coloured like the Light Green in all respects except that the colouring is broken with irregular patches of clear yellow. The yellow areas are usually confined to a head patch, flights, secondaries, and tail feathers, and a broken area on the chest from wing butt to wing butt. If this clear area on the chest is narrow and clear-cut the bird is called Banded Pied and if wide,

Deep-Green
Cinnamon

Cobalt–
Cinnamon

Cinnamon

39

broken, and irregular it is known as Dominant Pied. The beak of the Dominant Pied Light Green is yellowish horn-colour, and the feet and legs can be pinkish flesh colour, blue, or a mixture of both.

The Dominant Pied Dark Green and Dominant Pied Olive Green are marked like the Dominant Pied Light Green except that the body colours are bright dark green and rich olive-green. There can be a Dominant Pied form of all the existing Green-series birds.

Dominant Pied Sky Blue is marked and coloured like the Sky Blue in all respects except that the colouring is broken with irregular patches of clear white. The white areas are usually confined to a head patch, flights, secondaries, and tail feathers, and a broken area on the chest from wing butt to wing butt. If this clear area on the chest is narrow and clear-cut the bird is called Banded Pied and if wide, broken, and irregular, it is known as Dominant Pied. The beak of the Dominant Pied Sky Blue is yellowish horn-colour, and the feet and legs are pinkish flesh colour, blue, or a mixture of both. There can be a Dominant Pied form of all the existing Blue-series birds.

The Dominant Pied Cobalt and Dominant Pied Mauve are both marked like the Dominant Pied Sky Blue except that their body colours are bright cobalt and rich dark mauve.

The clear-flighted Greens are similar in colouring to the above-mentioned birds. Here, however, the pattern is more precise, although there can be a variation in the quality of the patterning. Clear-flighted Light Green is marked and coloured like the Light Green in all respects except for a clear yellow head patch, clear flights and tail. The beak of the Clear-flighted Light Green is horn-coloured and the feet and legs are greyish-blue but can be pinkish.

Clear-flighted Dark Green and Clear-flighted Olive Green are marked the same as the Clear-flighted Light Green except that the body colours are dark green and olive-green. There can be a Clear-flighted form of all the existing Green-series birds.

Clear-flighted Sky Blue is marked and coloured like the Sky Blue in all respects except for a clear white head patch, clear flights and tail. The beak of the Clear-flighted Sky Blue is horn-coloured and the feet and legs are bluish.

The Clear-flighted Cobalt and Clear-flighted Mauve are both marked in the same way as the Clear-flighted Sky Blue except that the body colours are cobalt and mauve.

Another character that causes an alteration in body colours like the

Dominant Pied
Light Green

Dominant Pied
Sky Blue

Dominant Pied

Slate Light Green

Grey is the Slate which exists in both the Green and the Blue series. However, it is only in the Blue-series birds that the slate colouring is clearly seen. Slate Light Green has a yellow forehead and mask which is ornamented on each side of the face with dull dark-violet cheek patches. On the lower part of the mask are six round black throat spots, one on each side partially hidden by the cheek patch. From the mask to the base of the tail, including rump, flanks, and thighs, the colour is hard dark green. On the back of the head, neck, mantle, back, and wings are dull-black undulating markings on a yellow ground. The flight feathers are blackish and the two long central tail feathers are dull deep blue. The remainder are yellow with dark pattern markings. The beak of the Slate Light Green is horn-coloured, and the feet and legs are blackish.

Slate Dark Green and Slate Olive Green are both marked like the Slate Light Green except for the change of body shade to a deep, even, dark green, and a dull, even, dark olive-green. The Slate Green forms are rather difficult to distinguish from the Violet Green birds. There can be Slate Green forms of all the other existing Green-series birds.

Slate Sky Blue has a white forehead and mask which is ornamented on each side of the face with dull, dark-violet cheek patches. On the lower part of the mask are six round black throat

Slate Sky Blue

Slate-Mauve

43

spots, one on each side partially hidden by the cheek patch. From the mask to the base of the tail, including the rump, flanks, and thighs, the colour is warm, slate-blue. On the back of the head, neck, mantle, back, and wings are black undulating markings on a white ground. The flight feathers are blackish and the two long central tail feathers are dull dark blue. The beak of the Slate Sky Blue is horn-coloured, and the feet and legs are blackish.

The Slate Cobalt and Slate Mauve are both marked like the Slate Sky Blue except that the body colours are dark slate-blue and blackish-slate. The Slate Mauve is the darkest of all the colours and therefore nearest so far to the desired black. Although similar in colour to the Greys their warm tone makes their body shades somewhat more attractive. There can be a Slate Blue form of all the existing Blue-series birds.

All the colours so far mentioned in this chapter have dark eyes with light iris rings. The varieties I will now be discussing all have eyes of a different colour.

Danish Recessive Pied Light Green is marked and coloured like the Light Green except that the colouring is heavily broken with irregular patches of clear rich yellow. The yellow usually covers about 60 per cent of the plumage and the green is of a particularly bright and clear colour. The cheek patches are broken with silvery-white, and the throat spots can be from one to a complete set. The beak is orange-yellow, and the feet and legs pink. The outstanding feature of this variety is that their eyes are a deep solid plum colour without the light iris ring, common to all the other varieties.

Danish Recessive Pied Dark Green and Danish Recessive Pied Olive Green are marked like the Danish Recessive Pied Light Green except for the change of body shade to rich dark green and deep olive-green. The yellow areas are correspondingly deeper in tone.

Danish Recessive Pied Sky Blue is marked and coloured like the Sky Blue except that the colouring is heavily broken with irregular patches of clear white. The cheek patches are broken with silvery-white and the throat spots can be from one to a complete set. The beak is orange-yellow and the feet and legs pink. The outstanding feature of this variety is that their eyes are a deep solid plum colour without the light iris rings common to all other varieties.

Danish Recessive Pied Cobalt and Danish Recessive Pied Mauve are marked like the Danish Recessive Pied Sky Blue except for the change of body shade to bright rich cobalt and dark pinkish-mauve. With all the Danish Pied varieties, both in the

Danish Recessive Pied Light Green

Danish Recessive Pied Sky Blue

Danish Recessive Pieds

45

Green and the Blue series, the ceres of the cock birds are purplish flesh-coloured and not the bright, solid blue of the other varieties.

Related to the Danish Recessive Pieds are the Dark-eyed Clear Yellow and Dark-eyed Clear White. Both these have the deep plum-coloured eyes without the light iris ring, and the whole of the plumage is pure yellow, or pure white, respectively. The depth of the pure yellow colouring of the Dark-eyed Clear Yellow varies according to whether the bird is masking light green, dark green, or olive-green. The beaks of the Dark-eyed Clear variety are orange-yellow, the ceres of the cocks purplish flesh-coloured, and the feet and legs pink.

I come now to three races of budgerigars that have red eyes — the Lutino and Albino, the Lacewing and the Fallow. The Lutino is clear yellow throughout with a slight trace of greenish suffusion on the rump and flanks when viewed at an angle in certain lights. Again the depth of the yellow shade differs according to the green colour being masked. The eyes are red with a light iris ring, the beak deep-yellowish horn-colour, the cere of the cock is purplish flesh-colour, and the feet and legs are pink.

   The Albino is clear white throughout with a slight trace of bluish

Lutino

White Lacewing

Fallow Sky Blue

47

suffusion on the rump and flanks when viewed at an angle in certain lights. The eyes are red with a light iris ring, the beak deep-yellowish horn-colour, the cere of the cock is purplish flesh-colour, and the feet and legs are pink.

Lacewing Yellow has a yellow forehead and mask which is ornamented on each side of the face with light pinkish-violet cheek patches. On the lower part of the mask are six round cinnamon-brown throat spots, one on each side is partially hidden by the cheek patch. From the mask to the base of the tail, including the rump, flanks, and thighs, the colour is clear yellow with a slight greenish suffusion. On the back of the head, neck, mantle, back, and wings, are soft cinnamon-brown undulating markings on a yellow ground. The flight feathers are cinnamon-brown and the two long central tail feathers are deep cinnamon with a tinting of dark blue. The beak of the Lacewing Yellow is yellowish horn-colour, the eyes are red with a light iris ring, the cere of the cock is purplish flesh-colour, and the feet and legs are pink.

The Lacewing form of the Dark Green and Olive form is of a considerably darker yellow shade. Sometimes the Olive form has a distinctive orange hue.

Lacewing White has a white forehead and mask which is ornamented on each side of the face with light pinkish-violet cheek patches. On the lower part of the mask are six round cinnamon-brown throat spots, one on each side is partially hidden by the cheek patch. From the mask to the base of the tail, including the rump, flanks, and thighs, the colour is clear white with a faint bluish suffusion. On the back of the head, neck, mantle, back, and wings are soft cinnamon-brown undulating markings on a white ground. The flight feathers are cinnamon-brown and the two long central tail feathers are deep cinnamon with a tinting of dark blue. The beak of the Lacewing White is yellowish horn-colour, the eyes are red with a light iris ring, the cere of the cock is purplish flesh-colour, and the feet and legs are pink.

The third member of the red-eyed group of budgerigars is the Fallow. There are two kinds of Fallows but they differ only in the colour of their eyes. German Fallows have red eyes with a light iris ring, whereas the English Fallows have red eyes which are solid and without the light iris ring. This being so, only one colour description will be necessary to cover both varieties.

Fallow Light Green has the forehead and mask rich yellow and this is ornamented on each side of the face with soft lilac cheek patches. On the lower part of the mask are six round brown throat spots, one on each side is partially hidden by the cheek patch. From the mask to the base of the tail is soft light greenish-yellow with the rump, flanks, and thighs having a more greenish tone. On the back of the head, neck, mantle, back, and wings are undulating markings ranging from cinnamon-brown to steel brown on a rich yellow ground. The flight feathers are brown and the two long central tail feathers are deep brownish-blue. The beak of the Fallow Light Green is a deep orange-yellow colour, the cere of the cock is purplish flesh-colour, and the feet and legs are pink.

The Fallow Dark Green and Fallow Olive Green are marked like the Fallow Light Green except for the change of body shade to a rich, yellowish, dark green and deep orange-olive-green. Some of the Fallow Olive Greens show a particularly beautiful orange tone quite distinct from that carried by any other variety.

Fallow Sky Blue has a white forehead and mask which is ornamented on each side of the face with soft lilac cheek patches. On the lower part of the mask are six round, brown throat spots, one on each side is partially hidden by the cheek patch. From the mask to the tail is soft whitish-blue with the rump, flanks, and thighs having a more bluish tone. On the back of head, neck, mantle, back, and wings are undulating markings ranging from cinnamon-brown to steel brown on a white ground. The flight feathers are brown, and the two long central tail feathers are deep brownish-blue. The beak of the Fallow Sky Blue is a deep orange-yellow colour, the cere of the cock is purplish flesh-colour, and the feet and legs are pink.

The Fallow Cobalt and Fallow Mauve are marked like the Fallow Sky Blue except for the change of body shade to soft whitish-cobalt with a pinkish tinge and soft pinkish-mauve.

In all the Blue-series birds that exist there can be Yellow-faced forms. There are several different kinds of this Yellow-faced Blue mutation which give varying amounts of yellow colouring on blue birds. The amount of yellow shown can vary from just the forehead, mask, wing butts, and tail to a completely yellowish overlay. It is obvious that with the vast number of Blue-series birds some beautifully coloured examples with yellow faces can be produced.

Except for a number of unestablished colours that appear periodically, and may be in the process of being developed, there now remain only the Crested kinds to be explained.

The Crested birds can be produced in all colours and with three different types of crest. The Full Circular Crest is like that carried by the Crested canaries with the head feathers radiating from the centre forming a complete circle. The Half Circular Crest is similar in design but only falling to the front of the head making a half-circular fringe. With the Tufted Crest the feathers form a tuft at the front of the head, something like that of the cockatiel only shorter. In the next chapter the manner in which the Crest and all other varieties are produced will be explained in an easy-to-understand manner.

Colours and how they can be produced

Before discussing the inheritance of the many varieties of budgerigars a few simple facts must be explained. Each bird is an individual with a complete set of chromosomes and their associated genes which control every aspect of the bird. These chromosome pairs exist in a given number and each member of each pair has its own quota of genes which can and does vary. All the sperms of the cock have a complete half-set of that bird's chromosomes, and all the ova of the hen likewise carry a complete half-set of chromosomes. When an ovum is fertilized by a sperm a complete set of chromosome pairs is reassembled and a new bird is made. All chromosomes are of pairs of equal size except the one that governs the sex. With cock birds the sex chromosome pairs are equal in size and called XX but the hen's pair consists of one X like the cock's and one Y which is small and carries no genes. The sole purpose of the Y is to determine the sex of the bird. The Y is not designed to carry any characters. The genes can be dominant, recessive, or intermediate in their behaviour and if carried on the X chromosome they are sex-linked.

I will now give some examples of how the colour characters carried by the birds are inherited and governed by rules known as the Mendelian principles of inheritance. With the dominant colour characters, birds carrying them on one half of a chromosome pair will show those colours as well as if they were on both sides. Recessive colours, on the other hand, will only reveal their presence when carried on both halves of the chromosome pair. Because colour characters can be carried in a number of different chromosome pairs, a bird can be one colour and carry in its genetic make up one or more colours, which it does not itself exhibit.

When a pure Green is mated to a pure Blue all the resulting young are green in colour but because they have a Blue parent they have the potential, when given the right mates, of reproducing further Blues. When birds have different-coloured parents as described above they are called Green split Blues (Green/Blue).

There is no visual difference in the green-coloured birds in matings 3 and 4; their genetic make up can only be discovered by test pairings with Blues.

Other matings can be calculated by using these rules and simply changing the colours: whenever Green-series birds are crossed

Mating colour table

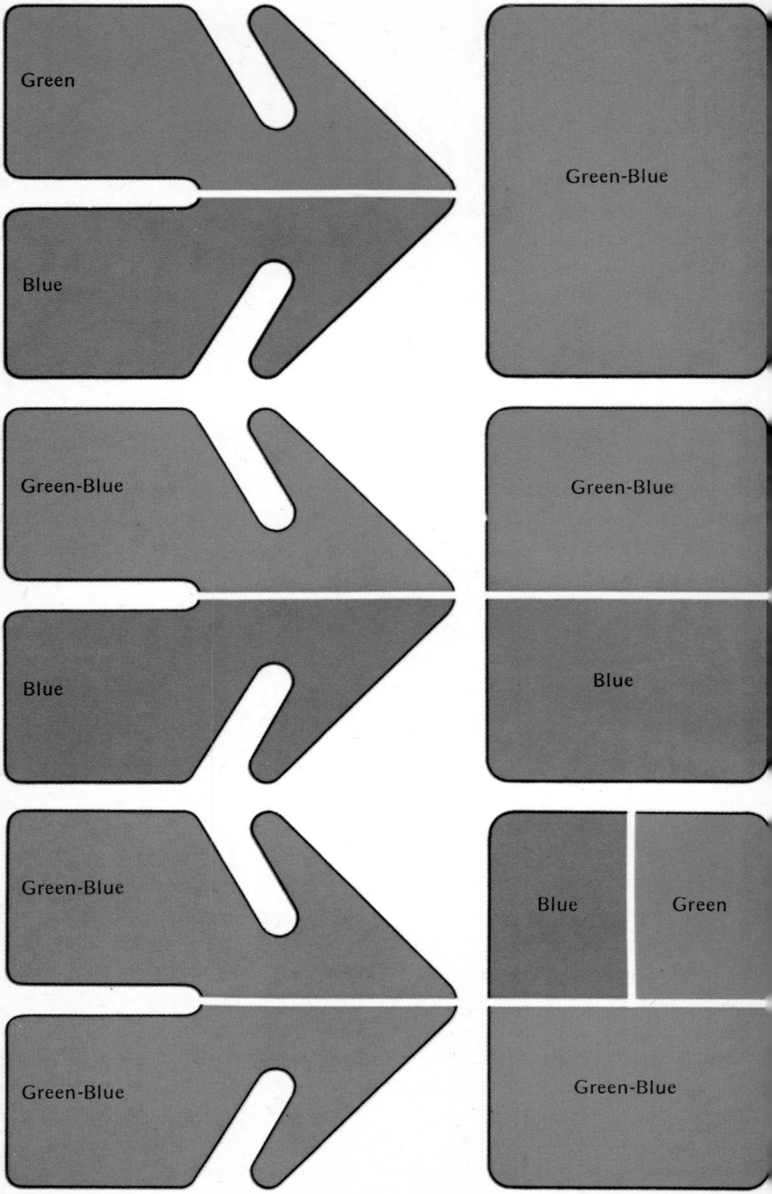
Green
Blue
Green-Blue
Green-Blue
Blue
Green-Blue
Blue
Green-Blue
Green-Blue
Blue
Green
Green-Blue

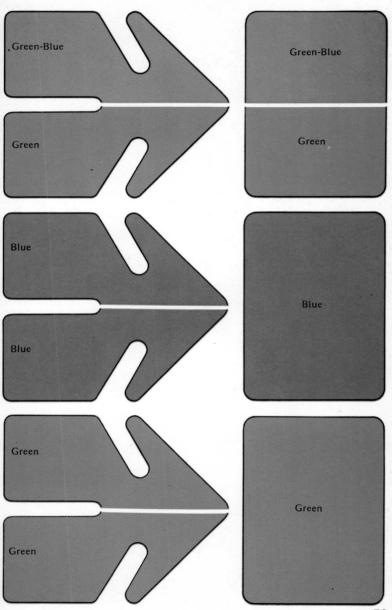

Green-Blue

Green

Green-Blue

Green

Blue

Blue

Blue

Green

Green

Green

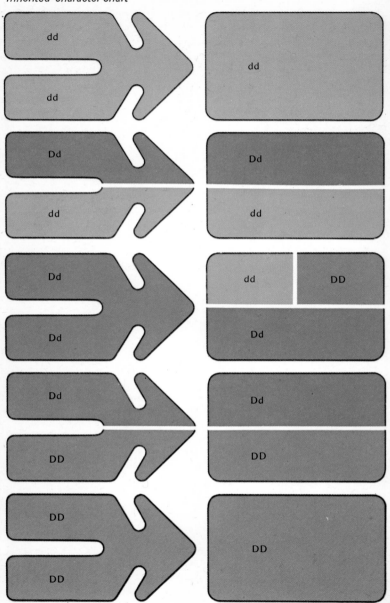

with Blue-series the expectations are the same except for the actual shade of green or blue. With individual crosses the percentages may vary somewhat, but when a number of the same cross is taken together the percentages will be found correct.

The depth of the colour carried by any variety is controlled by an inherited character called Dark (D) and although not a colour itself its presence changes the colour shade. The Dark character works independently of any other colour character that may be in a bird's genetic make up. The complete absence gives the basic colour shade of light green and sky blue; its presence in a single quantity (Dd) gives the dark green and cobalt colours; but when in double quantity (DD) the olive-green and mauve tones result.

I have now shown how the Green, Blue, and Dark characters are inherited and these have a bearing on all varieties. I will now deal with some other colour characters which have their own visual expressions. The colour varieties known as the Dominants are Grey, Violet, Australian Pied, and Continental Clear-flight. The first two alter the colour forming plumage patterns. The Grey character, which is as effective in single as double quantity, causes the Green series to take on a mustard-grey-green shade and the Blue series battleship-grey tones. A Grey single quantity paired to a Blue will give young of each colour in equal proportions. Similarly a Grey Green single quantity to a Green gives the same proportions. These two basic crosses are the ones most frequently used by breeders of the Grey-series birds. There can be a Grey and Grey Green form of all the other colours and varieties, each having its own particular shade of Grey or Grey Green.

The Violet character operates in the same way as the Grey except that the beautiful vivid violet colouring is only visible when Blue and a single Dark character are together with the Violet. If Violet is added to an ordinary Sky Blue then Violet Sky Blues result and such birds have a bright pale-cobalt shade. By adding Violet and Mauve the resulting birds are Violet Mauves having a deep warm violet-mauve shade. When a single or double quantity of the Violet character is added to a Blue-series bird having a single quantity of the Dark character, i.e. a Cobalt, then the Violet Cobalt (Visual Violet) is produced.

The Violet birds in these theoretical matings have the character in a single quantity only. This is true of the majority of birds used for breeding. There can also be Violet forms of the Green-series birds and here the presence of the character in their genetic make up causes them to have an altered shade of green. Violet Greens as

Violet breeding table

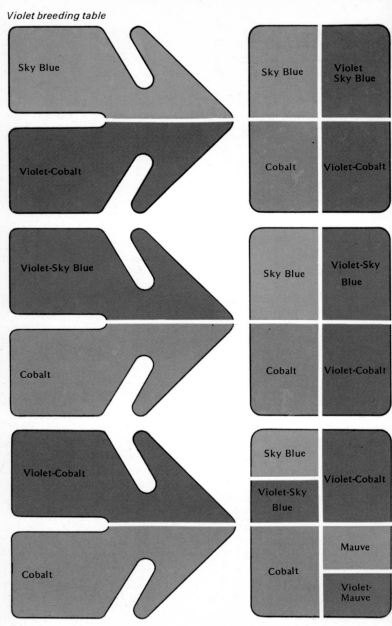

Sky Blue	Violet Sky Blue
Cobalt	Violet-Cobalt

Sky Blue	Violet-Sky Blue
Cobalt	Violet-Cobalt

Sky Blue / Violet-Sky Blue	Violet-Cobalt
Cobalt	Mauve / Violet-Mauve

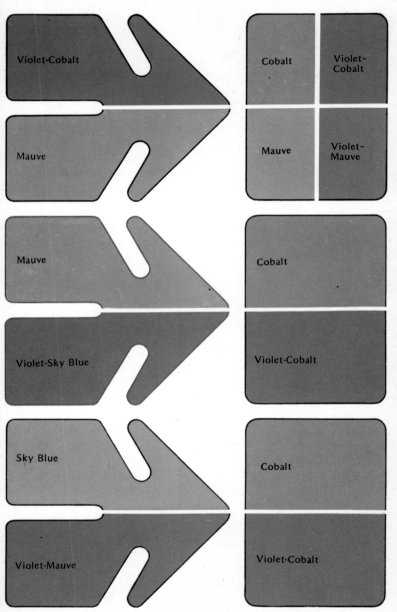

57

they are called can be useful in the breeding quarters as they help to enrich the colour of the Visual Violets they produce. Obviously by using Green birds the number of Visual Violets produced from these matings is less than it would be if blue-coloured birds had been used. It is possible to breed Violet forms of all other varieties both in their Green and Blue series.

I have just explained the breeding behaviour of two Dominant characters that cause a change of the colour shade, and now I pass to another — where the pattern of the colours is altered. Australian Pieds, now known as Dominant Pieds, are in all varieties with their plumage broken by irregular areas of yellow or white. They can have either a single or double quantity of the Pied character, both of which show the same visual effect. Most birds are single factor as the majority of Dominant Pieds are bred from one Pied and one non-Pied parent. Other colour characters carried by the Pieds do not affect the pattern but only the colour. A Dominant Pied single character paired to any non-Pied will give half Dominant Pieds and half non-Pied young. For instance, a Dominant Pied single character Light Green paired to a Sky Blue gives Dominant Pied Light Green/Blue and Light Green/Blue, or a Dominant Pied single-character Mauve paired to a White Sky Blue gives Dominant Pied Cobalt White and Cobalt/White. From this it will be seen how easy it is to work out the expectations from Dominant Pied matings. It is not wise to cross Dominant Pieds with other varieties such as Albinos, Lutinos, Lacewings, or Recessive Pieds since the Dominant Pied forms of these are not satisfactory from the colour angle.

The next Dominants are the Continental Clear-flights which again can be had in single or double quantity, both showing the same visual colouring. Continental Clear-flights can be had in the Green and Blue series of all the other varieties except of course the Pied kinds where their pattern markings would not be visible. Like the Dominant Pied, the Clear-flights are mostly single-character birds and therefore a Clear-flight paired with a Normal gives half Clear-flight and half Normal young. The expression of the Clear-flight character can be extremely varied, including anything from a bird with only a head spot to the over-marked kind. Clear-flights have another special breeding property and when combined with the Danish Recessive Pied a completely new type is evolved — the Dark-eyed Clears which I shall be discussing later in this chapter.

The sex-linked breeding kinds consist of Albinos (Lutinos),

Dominant Pied crossbreeding

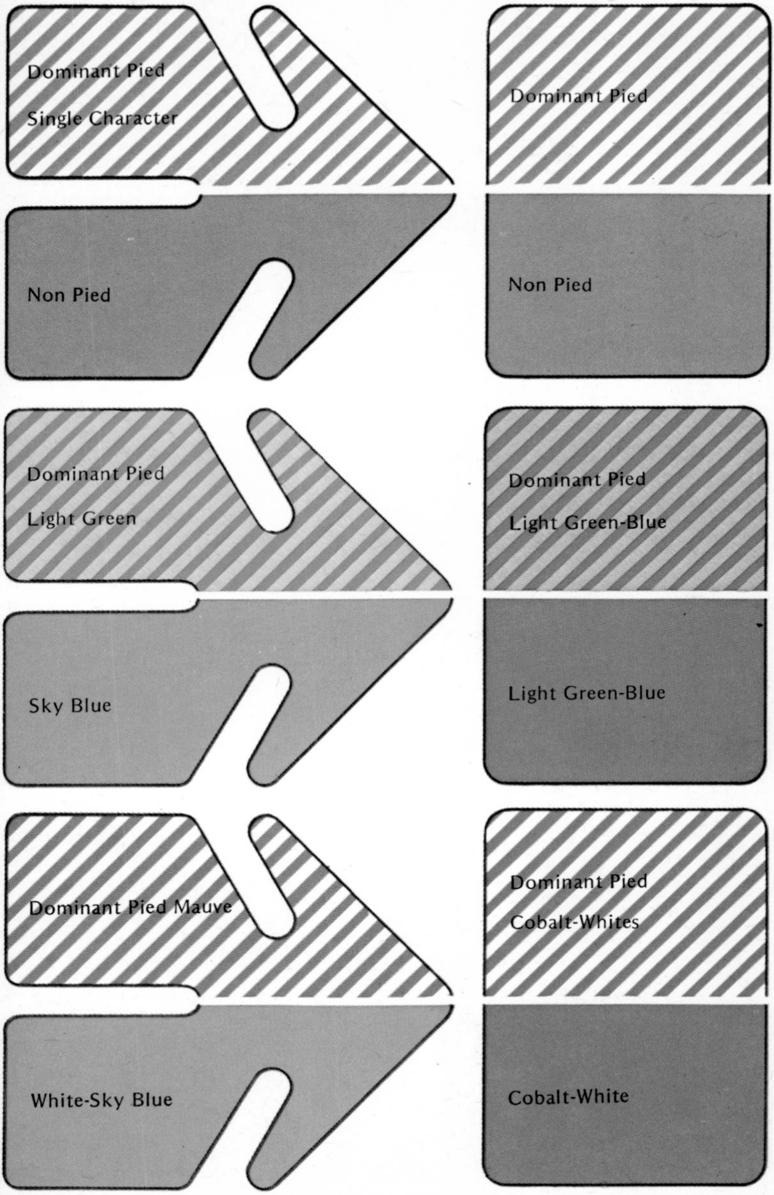

Dominant Pied
Single Character

Non Pied

Dominant Pied

Non Pied

Dominant Pied
Light Green

Sky Blue

Dominant Pied
Light Green-Blue

Light Green-Blue

Dominant Pied Mauve

White-Sky Blue

Dominant Pied
Cobalt-Whites

Cobalt-White

Sex-link table

60

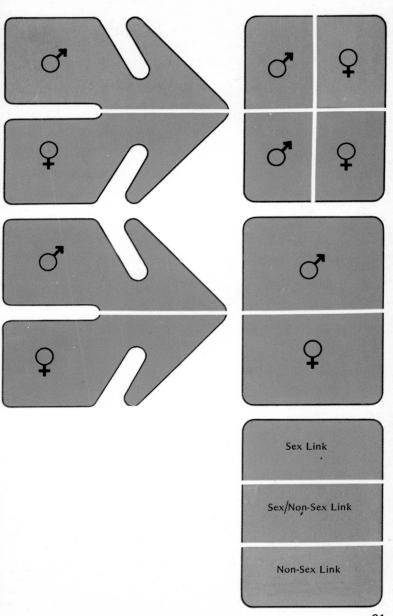

61

Cinnamons, Opalines, Slates, and Lacewings, all having different colour expressions with the same breeding behaviour. When the reader is conversant with the simple mathematics of sex-linked inheritance it is easy to work out the expectations of any of these varieties.

When two different varieties of sex-linked birds are paired together one acts as though it were a normal non-linked bird. For instance, if a Cinnamon cock is paired to an Opaline hen the young will be Non-linked/Cinnamon Opaline cocks and Cinnamon hens. The reverse pairing of Opaline cock to a Cinnamon hen gives Non-linked/Cinnamon Opaline cocks and Opaline hens. These sex-linked rules can be used to work out all the various matings of the five sex-linked varieties.

I now come to the Recessive kind consisting of Fallows, Danish Pieds, Greywings, Clearwings, Whites, and Yellows. Fallows as will have been seen in the colour descriptions have red eyes and there are two different breeding kinds. If these two kinds of Fallows are paired together all their young have normally coloured eyes although both parents have red. This fact shows that the two forms owe their existence to quite separate mutations. When either kind is paired to a Normal all the young are normally coloured but still carry the Fallow character. A 'split' Fallow paired to a Fallow gives half Fallows and half 'split' Fallows. There can be Fallow kinds of all the Green- and Blue-series birds. Some most interestingly coloured specimens can be evolved by using the Fallow character in producing composite varieties.

The plum-eyed Danish Pieds are Recessive like the Fallows and when paired to other Green and Blue varieties give only normally coloured young, all 'split' for Danish Pied. When paired to Continental Clear-flights they give Clear-flights and Normals 'split' for Recessive Pied as would be expected from such a cross. The Clear-flight/Danish Pied back-crossed to Danish Recessive Pied gives an unusual result of Clear-flight, Normal, Recessive Pied, and Dark-eyed Clears. These Dark-eyed Clears have the plum-coloured eyes of the Danish Pieds with pure-yellow or pure-white plumage throughout. To date no reason has been found for the appearance of these all-clear birds but it is known that they give Clear-flight and Normal young when mated to Normals. This indicates that they are, in fact, the Danish Pied form of the Clear-flight and that the crossing of the two different Pied characters gives Dark-eyed Clear birds. Danish Recessive Pieds paired to Dominant Pieds and the Dominant/Recessive Pieds paired back to Recessive Pieds do not

62

Danish Pied crossbreeding

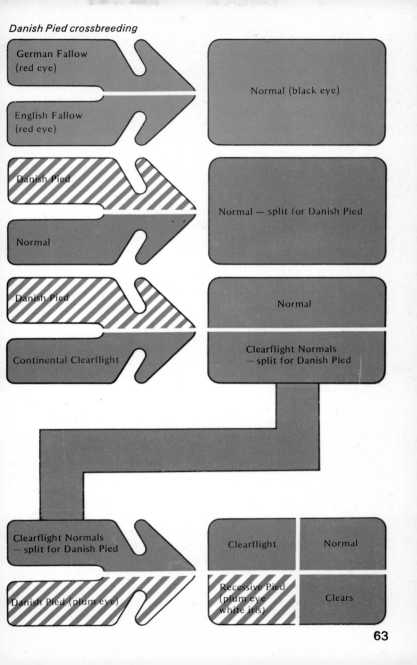

German Fallow (red eye) + English Fallow (red eye) → Normal (black eye)

Danish Pied + Normal → Normal — split for Danish Pied

Danish Pied + Continental Clearflight → Normal / Clearflight Normals — split for Danish Pied

Clearflight Normals — split for Danish Pied + Danish Pied (plum eye) → Clearflight | Normal | Recessive Pied (plum eye white iris) | Clears

give any perfectly clear birds, this being peculiar to the Clear-flight/Danish Recessive Pied cross.

Greywings, Clearwings, Whites, and Yellows form an interesting group, all being Recessive to Normal colours. Yellows and Whites are Recessive to Greywings and Clearwings both of which can be 'split' for Yellow or White. However when Greywings and Clearwings are paired together they give birds which are a combination of both kinds and are known as Full Body Coloured Greywings. These birds have the usual grey undulations of the Greywings but with body colours of almost the same depth of colour as Normals. If a Full Body Coloured Greywing is paired to a Yellow or White the expectation is half Greywings and half Clearwings, all 'split' for Yellow or White of course. It is interesting that Normal birds cannot be 'split' for Greywing and White (or Yellow) at the same time or for both Greywing and Clearwing or Clearwing and White (or Yellow).

In the foregoing paragraphs I have discussed the many interesting colours and varieties which exist in present-day budgerigars. But there still remain to be discussed all the Blue-series varieties which can be produced in further forms showing various amounts of yellow on their white ground. These are the Yellow-face Blue series. There are a number of different mutations of which three can be clearly recognized. These are known as Mutant I and Mutant II. The former have yellow on face, wing butts, and tail, and the latter have a strong-yellow overlay over most of their plumage. The third member is called Golden-faced because of the rich, golden-yellow colour.

The breeding behaviour of the Yellow-faced Blue Mutant I is particularly interesting as the character differs in its inheritance from the other forms. Like all characters they can be carried by the birds in single or double quantities, but Mutant I is the only single-character bird that shows the yellow colouring. When birds have the Mutant I character in double quantity they resemble the ordinary blue-coloured specimens and have no trace of yellow.

Double-character birds are indistinguishable from the ordinary Blue series and it is only in their breeding results that their genetic make up is revealed. Yellow-faced Blue Mutant II follows the ordinary way of inheritance and both single- and double-quantity birds have the same colouring. A Yellow-faced single-character Sky Blue Mutant II paired with a Sky Blue gives 50 per cent of each kind and when two single Mutant II characters are paired together they give 25 per cent Sky Blues, 50 per. cent Yellow-faced single

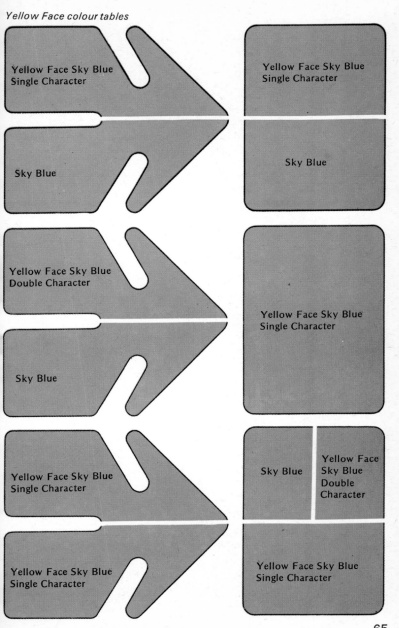

Yellow Face Sky Blue
Single Character

Sky Blue

Yellow Face Sky Blue
Single Character

Sky Blue

Yellow Face Sky Blue
Double Character

Sky Blue

Yellow Face Sky Blue
Single Character

Yellow Face Sky Blue
Single Character

Yellow Face Sky Blue
Single Character

Sky Blue

Yellow Face
Sky Blue
Double
Character

Yellow Face Sky Blue
Single Character

Yellowface
Cobalt-Cinnamon

Yellowface
Sky Blue

Yellowface

66

character Sky Blue Mutant II, and 25 per cent Yellow-faced double character Sky Blue Mutant II. The Golden-faced variety reproduces in the same way as Mutant II, the only difference being that the double-character birds have the finest colouring.

The brilliant and varied colouration of Yellow-faced Blue-series birds helps to create a particularly attractive composite form known as 'Rainbows'. These 'Rainbows' are the result of combining the Yellow-faced Blue, Opaline, and Clearwing characters in a single bird. There are many combinations of pairings that will give varying percentages of Yellow-faced Opaline Whitewings ('Rainbows'), such as Yellow-faced Opaline White cock to Whitewing hen, Opaline Whitewing cock to Yellow-faced White hen, Yellow-faced Opaline/Whitewing cock to Opaline Whitewing hen, Yellow-faced Opaline Whitewing cock to Opaline White hen etc. The best-coloured Yellow-faced Opaline Whitewings ('Rainbows') are the Cobalt and Violet Cobalt kinds and the Grey Slate and Mauve the least attractive.

There are a large number of composite varieties that can be bred and experimentation is not yet complete. There is tremendous scope for breeders to produce these interesting birds, but much will depend upon their ingenuity in combining the varieties. Colour breeding is a particularly fascinating aspect of budgerigar breeding and combined with exhibiting makes the hobby appealing to bird lovers of all ages.

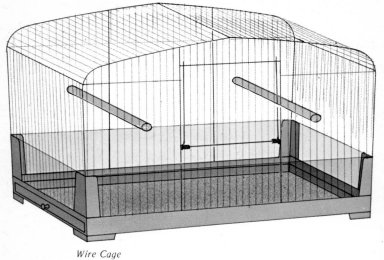

Wire Cage

Accommodation

One of the attractions of budgerigars is that they can be kept and bred both in and out of doors provided certain standards are maintained. Fit, healthy budgerigars can bear quite cold weather conditions without discomfort providing that they are well fed, and their housing is dry and draught free. Budgerigars can be kept in cages, pens, and aviaries, depending on the purpose for which they are required and the accommodation available to the owner.

For the tame household pet bird all-wire, or wire-and-plastic, cages are the most suitable. Excellent, roomy, well-designed cages can be bought from good pet stores. The other type of cage, known as a box cage, consists of a wire-fronted wooden box. This is normally used for housing breeding and exhibition stock. These box cages are best made in tiered blocks and divided by wooden slides. The slides can be removed to make a spacious flight cage for the birds during the non-breeding period. The size of these breeding cages will depend to some extent on the space available in the bird room but should not be less than 3ft. long, 18in. high, and 15in. deep. Such cages can be bought complete with all accessories, or can be made up by the breeder to suit special requirements.

A bird room to hold these cages can be specially constructed, or existing buildings can be converted to make suitable bird rooms. These buildings should be airy, dry, free from draughts, and have plenty of natural light. Electric lighting is useful for feeding the birds on dark mornings and evenings but this is not essential. A bird room should, if possible, be large enough to allow for one or two wire pens in which to keep young stock when removed from their parents. It also enables the birds to exercise and fly freely. Again the size of these pens will depend on the building itself, but if possible two should be constructed so that cocks and hens can be kept separately when not breeding.

Pens are, in fact, small aviaries to hold one breeding pair of birds, and can be either with or without flights. Single-pair flighted breeding pens are undoubtedly the best way in which to control breed budgerigars : they combine the freedom of an aviary with the control of a cage. If flighted pens are not possible then the un-flighted ones are the best for control breeding. The size of each pen should be approximately 2ft. wide, 4½ft. long, and 6ft. high, and if flights are attached they can be of the same dimensions. The number of pens constructed will be governed by the breeding

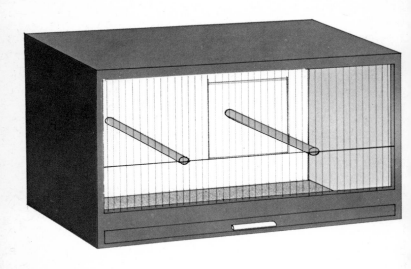

Box Cage

requirements of the owner and the accommodation available.

Aviaries are buildings in which a number of pairs are flying to-gether, either for colony breeding or for resting the stock during the non-breeding periods. A well-designed aviary containing different-coloured budgerigars will add life and colour to any garden and give considerable pleasure to the owner. Aviaries should consist of a sleeping and feeding shelter with an open all-wire flight approxi-mately twice the area of the shelter portion. The actual design of the building must rest with the owner if it is to be an entirely new building but an aviary can be made from another structure that is adapted for the purpose.

Perches in pens and aviaries must be firmly fixed and placed clear of all water, seed, and grit vessels. They can be made of machined wooden dowelling, or natural branches from such trees as apple, pear, plum, cherry, hazel, hawthorn, elm, or beech. Natural wood perches do help to make aviaries more decorative and undoubtedly the birds get great benefit and delight from gnawing the wood. It is not possible to grow trees or shrubs successfully in flights as the powerfully beaked budgerigars nibble the buds as they develop thus killing the plants.

All aviaries and bird rooms should be vermin proof. This can be done by placing strips of small mesh wire netting round the bottom. If the floors are wooden the aviaries should be raised on stone or brick blocks so that any attempts by vermin to gnaw their way in can be detected and remedied. Concrete, brick, or stone-slab bird-room floors are best covered with vynyl or some similar plastic material as this helps to maintain an even temperature and is easy to clean. The floors of pens and aviaries are best covered with a layer of sand, coarse sawdust, or a mixture of these, thus making cleaning easier. Flight floors can be covered with sand or fine gravel, or various kinds of grasses can be planted to give more decoration. If grasses are used, strips underneath the main perching areas should be cut out and filled in with gravel, this again is an aid to cleaning.

Budgerigars do not normally bath in the same way as finch-like birds but they do enjoy rolling in damp grass and their owners will get great delight from watching them at play. All windows should be made to open for ventilating purposes and must be covered on the inside with small-mesh wire screens to prevent the birds escaping or harming themselves by flying into the glass. Food and water vessels can be made of glass, china, earthenware, metal, or plastic. They should be placed on a shelf at the side of the shelters, or on a small, raised platform, so that they are clear of the floor.

Aviary

72

Water can be given in flat dishes or fountains which can be obtained from bird stores. Fountains are very useful in large flighted aviaries if the water cannot be changed every day. If the owner has a large collection of budgerigars and does not wish to refill seed vessels daily the seed can be given in automatic hoppers, obtainable in a number of different sizes. From these notes it will be seen that bird keepers can make their bird rooms and aviaries look very attractive.

General feeding

The budgerigar is as easy to feed as it is to house. Their diet consists mainly of millet and canary seeds blended in different proportions to suit individual studs of birds. Packets of ready-blended seeds can now be bought from most pet shops, but if more than two pairs of budgerigars are kept it is more economical to buy loose seeds from the bird stores. Such seeds can be bought already blended in different mixtures or separately so they can be mixed to the owner's requirements. When dealing with as many as ten or twelve pairs of birds the blended seed mixtures are the most economical to buy and store. For the owner who likes to mix the bird seeds the following all-the-year-round mixture is very good: two parts small canary, one part large canary, two parts white millet, half part yellow millet, half part panicum millet. A few whole oats or groats can be added, and the amount increased during the breeding period.

Millet sprays are useful tit-bits for both cage and aviary specimens and can be used to encourage birds to settle down in stock or show cages. Budgerigars that are a little off-colour will often eat millet sprays when they will not take their ordinary seed mixture. Some birds will eat a little kelp or linseed. These seeds contain oils which are particularly beneficial during the cold weather, but should only be given in limited quantities as they are of a fattening nature.

Green foods are an important part of the diet as they supply the birds with fresh, natural vitamins. Green foods should be given regularly and there are many varieties from which to choose. Some varieties of greens are of course eaten more readily but when their favourite sorts are not available they will eat some of the other kinds. Seeding grasses (not the hairy spikey kinds), chickweed, and spinach are favoured by most budgerigars and are obtainable most of the year. Other green foods that can be eaten by budgerigars are shepherd's purse, seeding heads of plaintains, sowthistles, young dandelion leaves, watercress, endives, chicory, Brussels sprouts, heart of cabbage, kale, carrots whole, sliced, or grated, and sweet apple. Further valuable green foods are sprouted seeds and cereals such as canary, millet, oats, wheat, and barley. These grains should be put into shallow dishes and soaked in cold water for twenty-four to forty-eight hours. The surplus water should then be drained and the dishes put in a warm place and left until the shoots are about 1/8th of an inch long. They will then be ready

Millet

Cuttlefish

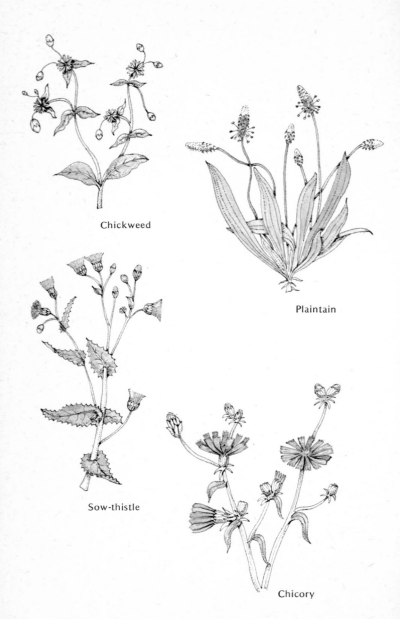

Chickweed

Plaintain

Sow-thistle

Chicory

for the birds. If the dishes of seeds are prepared on different days a constant supply is available.

A certain amount of soft food is also beneficial for budgerigars. This can be in the form of canary cod-liver-oil food, insectivorous food, a mixture of these two, or specially prepared budgerigar food. Cubes of wholemeal bread moistened with water, or milk, will be found acceptable to most birds. All these foods can be given periodically during the non-breeding times, and small quantities given daily when there are chicks in the nest. It is extremely important that any food that is not eaten should be removed at the end of the day. Owners should remember that stale or mouldy soft food will quickly upset the birds and can lead to serious complications.

In addition to their seed, water, and green food, all budgerigars, whether housed in cages, pens, or aviaries, need a constant supply of grits and minerals. Grits are for assisting the birds to grind their food into a consistency so that it can be assimilated into their systems. As these small sharp-edged pieces wear they are voided by the birds and have to be replaced. This is a continuous process all through their lives. One of the most important mineral elements is lime (calcium) which is the main component of cuttlefish bone. Besides giving the birds the required lime, the act of nibbling at the cuttlefish bone helps to keep the beaks of the birds at the required length. Other good sources of lime and trace minerals are old mortar rubble, raw chalk, clean river and sea sand, and dried domestic hens' egg shells. There are also manufactured mineralized blocks which are easy to fix in the cage or aviary. The necessary grits can be bought in packets, or loose, from all good bird stores.

General breeding

Budgerigars are undoubtedly one of the simplest of cage and aviary birds to breed. Nevertheless certain procedures should be followed if the most satisfactory results are to be obtained. Only healthy, strong-flying, fully matured birds should be used in the breeding quarters, and unless the breeder is experienced, the pairing of related birds should be avoided. If birds in the above category are well housed and well fed the breeder should have little trouble in inducing most of them to mate, lay eggs, hatch, and rear strong, healthy chicks. There is no guarantee that any particular pair of birds will breed although the vast majority of them do.

Having settled on the type of accommodation and obtained the necessary breeding birds some time prior to the breeding season the newcomer will want to know the best time of year to pair up the birds. The most satisfactory breeding results are achieved if the selected birds are given their nesting boxes in late February or early March. Nesting boxes can be of many designs and can either be made by the breeder or obtained from bird stores. In colony breeding aviaries it is always best to hang the nest boxes at the same height. Allow two boxes for each pair. When the pairs have selected their boxes the unused ones can be removed and kept as replacements. When cage breeding not all the birds need be mated at the same time, but only when both members of the pair are seen to be in full breeding condition. When cock birds are in breeding condition their ceres are smooth, bright, and deep blue (except in the red-eyed and Recessive Pied varieties where they are purplish flesh-coloured) and those of all hens are rough and deep chocolate-brown. It is usual with fit birds for the hens to start laying their clutches fifteen to twenty days after being mated. The incubation time for each egg is seventeen to eighteen days. The eggs are laid on alternate days, so with a clutch of five there can be ten days between the hatching of the first and last eggs. Chicks leave the nest boxes when they are fully feathered and able to fly which is when they are about a month old. When the youngsters have been out of the nest for a week or so and are seen to be feeding on their own they should be taken away from their parents. This is to allow the adult birds to proceed with their second clutches of eggs unhampered by the first chicks.

Throughout the breeding season the birds require the kind of feeding described in Chapter 5 but in increased quantities to cope with the large appetites of the fast-growing young. When the

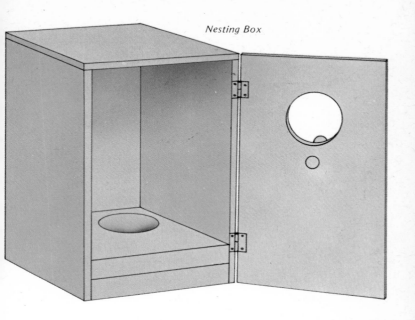

Nesting Box

young are about six to eight days old most breeders put closed coded year-dated metal rings on their legs as permanent marks of identification. These rings are obtainable through membership of the parent Budgerigar Society or one of its affiliated societies. It is advisable for anyone interested in budgerigars to become a member of at least one of these societies to get ring-code numbers, magazines, and various show benefits. Birds can also be rung with split metal or plastic rings but as these are easily removed they do not constitute an indisputable permanent record. Nevertheless coloured plastic rings are useful for identifying special birds or strains of birds in conjunction with the closed metal rings. Particulars of each breeding pair, and the ring numbers of the young they produce, should be entered in a stock book so that family histories can be traced back whenever required. This procedure will prevent close inbreeding and will help the breeder to trace any unusual colours should they appear in the nests.

In the early parts of this book I described the many different colour varieties of budgerigars and to which breeding group they belonged. I also showed how these colours are produced. Certain colours carry other colours hidden in their genetic make up. These

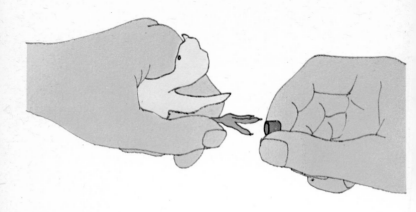

Fixing an identification ring to the leg of the bird

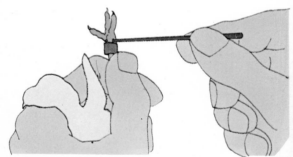

latent colours can be reproduced when given the right kind of mates.

From this it is clear that breeders can get a great deal of enjoyment from mating various colour crosses of the different varieties and their 'splits'. With careful thought and selection of the stock birds it is possible in the course of a few breeding seasons to evolve some quite spectacular composite birds. There are still a great many that have yet to be bred. Their production will, I know, appeal to the imagination of many experimental colour breeders.

Single household pets

Budgerigars are popular world-wide as household pets. They give endless pleasure and companionship to thousands of people of all ages. Not only do most budgerigars quickly become finger tame, but a very large proportion of them learn to repeat words and other sounds. It is this ability that makes them even more desirable as family pets. Budgerigars suitable for training as talking pets are reasonably cheap to buy, quite easy to feed, and, of course, can be kept in households where other pets are not suitable. The correct and most successful time to train a budgerigar is soon after it has left the care of its parents and can feed fully on its own. Some hen birds do learn to talk and become very tame, but young cock birds are much more reliable. It is a fallacy that birds must be kept in pairs. In fact a single budgerigar will become far more attached to its owner than it would if it had a companion.

I would suggest that the following procedure should be followed when it has been decided to have a pet budgerigar in the family circle. The bird should be ordered from either a local budgerigar breeder or pet-bird stores some time before the bird is required. The sex and choice of colour should be stated at the time of ordering so that the right bird can be selected. Although the colour of the bird has no bearing whatsoever on its talking ability it is more satisfactory if the purchaser does select a colour. Before the bird is obtained preparations for its arrival should be made by getting a roomy cage, a supply of seed, some millet sprays, a packet of grit, a piece of cuttlefish bone, and a mineral nibble. There are several well-known brands of packeted seeds available at bird stores and most larger supermarkets, and these are ideal for the single pet bird. The other requirements can be bought from bird stores together with the sand, or sanded sheets, for covering the bottom of the cage. The pet bird should be given a small piece of wholemeal bread from time to time, and a regular supply of green food such as chickweed, seeding grass, spinach, cabbage, or a piece of sweet apple or carrot. Sweets, cake, meat products, and other household foods should not be given to pet birds : although the bird may like to eat them they are not good for its general well-being.

When the bird first arrives it should be put into its cage together with food, water, grit etc. and placed in a quiet room so that it can settle down. The bird will probably be used to a different kind of food vessel, so it is advisable to sprinkle some seed on the cage floor near the seed pot. This will ensure that the bird does not go hungry during the first few hours in its new home. In the beginning it is advisable for only one member of the household to attend to the bird's care. Whenever the cage is approached the bird's chosen name should be spoken in a clear even tone, particularly when it is being given seed or green food as this is an important part of the training. After a few days the young bird will usually become accustomed to its instructor, and will be almost ready for finger training. The hand, holding a piece of millet spray, or green food, should be slowly put into the cage and kept very still whilst the bird comes forward to nibble at the offering. This should be repeated daily until the bird is no longer frightened and will hop onto the trainer's hand to get at the tit-bit. It is then only a matter of patience and perseverance before the bird is fully tame. By this time the bird may well be repeating its name quite freely. When this happens a few short sentences can be used in the training to increase its vocabulary. The next step is to allow the bird out of its cage to have flying exercise which will help to keep it in good bodily condition. Before the cage door is opened it is important to ensure that all doors and windows are firmly closed, any open heating covered by a guard, and flowers or pot plants removed from the room. The door of the cage should be left open so that the bird can come out when it is ready. On no account should it be forced to come out. Until the bird is fully trained it should be let out before being given its morning seed. The food can then be used to entice the bird back into the cage when it is hungry. The time and frequency of periods of flying exercise can be decided by the owner to fit the individual bird's requirements. With care it is not very long before the bird becomes a fully fledged, and much loved, member of the family.

Patience and care help to overcome the pet's timidity

Exhibiting

It is not uncommon for breeders of a few seasons' standing to exhibit their stock in competition with other breeders at local cage-bird shows. Exhibiting is an essential part of the fancy and helps to maintain and improve the overall quality of the breed through competition. Obviously there is more to exhibiting birds than putting them into show cages and taking them to shows. If the birds are kept in flights or aviaries they will need to be steadied down in stock cages, and trained to sit calmly in show cages.

The owner should first select the best of his stock and put them into cages, keeping the cocks and hens apart. The usual-sized breeding cages hold four to six exhibition birds, and should be used for steadying the birds. After a week or so their training in show-cage work can begin. The simplest way to do this is to hang show cages over the open door of the stock cages so that the birds have free access. They can be encouraged to enter the show cages if millet sprays or green food are put inside. When the birds have become used to the cages they can be shut in for an hour or two. The time should be gradually increased until they are quite happy at being in the show cages all day. When the birds appear to be quite at home even when the cages are moved and handled, they are ready for exhibiting. With show birds it is extremely important that all their feathers are complete and in a tight shiny condition and that there are no missing toenails or overlong nails. The general feather condition can be helped and improved by the periodic use of a fine spray and clean water. Any spraying should be done during the early part of the day so that the birds are thoroughly dry before nightfall. A special cage should be used for spraying the birds. It will prevent the stock cages getting wet, and the birds will dry more satisfactorily.

Before entering budgerigars for a show a schedule of classes and entry forms should be obtained from the show secretary. After reading the schedule and deciding which classes are applicable to the birds, the entry form should be completed and returned to the secretary, with the required entry fees. The birds entered in the show should be put into a clean show cage with plenty of seed on the floor the day before. They should be taken to the show hall in good time for the judging, and class labels should be stuck in the centre of the bottom rails of the show cages. Check to ensure the birds are in their correct classes. Any show successes should be entered in the stock register against the appropriate birds so that a permanent record is kept for reference. This record is often very useful when matching up pairs to produce exhibition stock.

When the birds are returned from a show they should be replaced in their stock cages and given millet sprays or some green food as an extra reward. The show cages themselves should be emptied of seed and water, cleaned and stored, ready for the next event; this procedure will preserve the show cages in a good and serviceable condition for many years.

Before showing budgerigars the intending exhibitor should first visit a few shows so that he will know what is required. Show officials are usually very helpful to newcomers, and willing to answer questions about show procedure, and other exhibitors will gladly discuss the show qualities of birds. Talking to other people interested in budgerigars is an excellent way to gain first-hand knowledge of this branch of the budgerigar fancy.

Show Cage

First aid

As a species budgerigars are hardy vigorous birds, not particularly prone to sickness. However, medical attention is sometimes needed. Any badly injured or very sick birds should have immediate veterinary attention. The conditions I shall be discussing in the next few paragraphs can be treated by the amateur bird keeper with simple remedies. When dealing with sick birds it is essential that the owner washes his hands both before and after touching each sick bird. Contagious diseases are passed on from one bird to another by their owners' failure to carry out this essential precaution.

Asthma. This is a respiratory condition that mainly affects household pets kept where the air conditions are steamy, overheated, or contaminated by gas or fumes from open fires or boilers. The symptoms are wheezing and difficulty in breathing but not accompanied by any mucus discharge from nostrils or beak. A bird suffering from these symptoms should be moved at once to an airy room of even temperature, and given one of the patent asthma cures.

Colds and chills. An affected bird will usually sit with its feathers puffed up, eyes watering, and occasionally sneezing. As soon as such symptoms are noted the bird should be caged on its own and taken into a warm even temperature. Six drops of syrup of buckthorn, or rosehip syrup, should be added to the drinking water that has first been boiled. If the bird is treated quickly enough it will usually recover within three or four days, and can be hardened off and returned to its usual cage or aviary. Should the condition be more advanced when first noticed Dianimol Syrup should be given as directed in place of the above-mentioned syrups.

Claws and beaks that are overlong. This condition is more likely to affect single pet birds than it is those who have the freedom of pens or aviaries. If claws are not clipped when they become overlong it is very easy for a bird to get caught up in the cage or aviary wirework and damage a toe, or even a leg. An overlong beak will prevent seed being eaten in the quantities necessary for good health. If the claws are examined in a strong light the vein ends can be clearly seen. The cuts should be made just below these veins to prevent bleeding. It is only the dry, extra length that should be clipped off the beak, cutting away from the bird. If the claw or beak

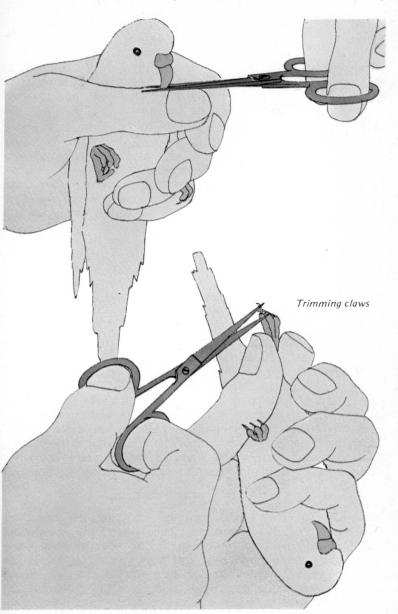

Trimming claws

bleeds a little after clipping it should be dabbed with an antiseptic lotion.

Constipation. If the bird is having trouble passing its droppings, some extra green food will quickly remedy the problem. It is fortunate that budgerigars rarely suffer from constipation.

Diarrhoea. This unpleasant condition can be caused by a bird eating stale or sour food, or it can be an aftermath of a neglected cold. A sick bird must be caged on its own and taken into a warm temperature of about 27 °C and given a course of Sulpha-methazine, 16 per cent solution, in drinking water that has first been boiled. This should be given for three days, then three days missed, and then given for one further day. The dosage is four drops to a tablespoonful of water. A sick bird should be given its normal seed, grit, and a millet spray, but all green food should be withheld until the bird recovers. This treatment usually clears the condition in a week. As soon as the droppings are normal again the bird can be returned to its usual quarters. The perches and seed and water vessels that have been in contact with the bird should be thoroughly washed with antiseptic and warm water.

Egg binding. The inability to pass a fully developed egg can affect very young, old, fat, overbred, or delicate hens. It can also be accentuated by cold weather conditions whilst a hen is laying a clutch of eggs. If a bird is noticed having difficulty in passing an egg she should be taken into the warmth and a few drops of olive oil applied to her vent with a camel hair brush. Usually after a few hours of warm conditions the egg will be passed and the bird will return to normal. However, the bird should be kept in the warmth for a day or two, and then hardened off and returned to the aviary or flight for a rest of some weeks before being used for breeding again.

Enteritis. This is similar to diarrhoea but more dangerous. The droppings are loose, greenish, bloodstained, and often foul smelling. A sick bird should be caged on its own and taken into a warm room. Advice should be sought from a veterinary surgeon as soon as possible because the disease could prove fatal if not treated in time. It is extremely important with this condition that everything that has been near the sick bird is thoroughly disinfected.

Feather plucking. Sometimes a hen will pluck the developing feathers from the neck, shoulders, and back of her growing young ones while they are in the next box. Unfortunately this bad hereditary habit cannot be cured, and it is not advisable to use the bird again for breeding purposes. Any offspring should also be excluded from future breeding plans as they too may carry the taint although they may regrow all their feathers.

French moult

French Moult. This is another hereditary feather condition. It can affect a few of the chicks or a whole nest in varying degrees. French Moult is a disease that causes the flight and tail feathers to fall out when the bird is nearing maturity. In bad cases some other feathers may also fall out. The exact cause of French Moult is not yet fully understood, but it is thought to be caused by the inability of the parent birds to pass on to their young certain essential feather-forming agents, or the inability of the young themselves to absorb these agents. Other factors such as breeding from birds that are too young, too old, too closely related, or have been used extensively for breeding or exhibiting purposes, can affect the severity of the condition. In the mild cases the feathers grow again, and the birds appear to be normal. But it is unwise to use these birds for breeding purposes, as they can pass the fault on to their young. When French Moult birds have recovered they can be used as pets, as can those that were feather plucked. There is no known cure for French

Moult and it does not occur if strong, healthy, unrelated birds from French Moult-free strains are used for breeding.

Red mite and grey lice. These insect pests are occasionally found in bird rooms and aviaries and can be disposed of quite easily by using a special spray.

Scaly Face. This is a condition caused by minute boring insects that attack the skin around the beak, eyes, feet, and legs. Its presence is usually first detected by whitish crumb-like growths that develop at the sides of the beak and push out the mask feathers. Fortunately there are several effective ointments and creams which if applied as directed will completely eradicate Scaly Face. As Scaly Face can be easily passed from one bird to another it is essential that before treatment all cages, perches, seed, and water vessels, and nest boxes that have been in contact with affected birds, should be thoroughly disinfected by washing with antiseptic and warm water.

Undershot beak

Undershot beaks. There are two forms of this malformation of the beak, one brought about by dirty feeding parents, and the other by an hereditary failing. The first cause can be seen in the nest when the birds' beaks become clogged with food. If a little olive oil is applied the accumulated food can gently be taken away. This may have to be done every day until the chicks are fairly well grown. The hereditary form is incurable as it is a defect in the structural formation of the beak.

Index

Distributors for
Bartholomew Pet Books

Australia

Book Trade : Tudor Distributors Pty. Limited, 14 Mars Road,
Lane Cove 2066, New South Wales, Australia

Canada

Pet Trade : Burgham Sales Ltd., 558 McNicoll Avenue,
Willowdale (Toronto), Ontario, Canada M2H 2E1
Book Trade : Clarke Irwin and Company, Limited,
791 St. Clair Avenue W., Toronto, Canada M6C 1B8

New Zealand

Pet Trade : Masterpet Products Limited,
7 Kaiwharawhara Road, Wellington, New Zealand
Book Trade : Whitcoulls Limited, Trade Department, Private Bag,
Auckland, Wellington, or Christchurch, New Zealand

South Africa

Book Trade : McGraw-Hill Book Company (S.A.) (Pty.) Limited,
P.O. Box 23423, Joubert Park, Johannesburg,
South Africa

U.S.A.

Pet Trade : Pet Supply Imports Inc., P.O. Box 497, Chicago,
Illinois, U.S.A.
Book Trade : The Two Continents Publishing Group Limited,
30 East 42nd Street, New York, N.Y. 10017, U.S.A.